FRETBOARD ROADMAPS JAZZ GUITAR

THE ESSENTIAL GUITAR PATTERNS THAT ALL THE PROS KNOW AND USE

BY FRED SOKOLOW

ISBN 0-634-00139-6

HAL•LEONARD®
CORPORATION

7777 W. BLUEMOUND RD. P.O. BOX 13819 MILWAUKEE, WI 53213

Visit Hal Leonard Online at
www.halleonard.com

CONTENTS

INTRODUCTION

Jazz is harmonically sophisticated and complex. Yet accomplished jazz guitarists can listen to a song they've never heard and, after one time around the chord progression, jump in and improvise solos or backup. They can do this in any key—all over the fretboard. They know several different soloing approaches and may never play the same solo twice.

There are moveable patterns on the guitar fretboard that make it possible to do these things "automatically" (there's no time to stop and figure out the math when you're jamming). The pros are aware of these "fretboard roadmaps," even if they don't read music. If you want to play jazz with other players, this is essential guitar knowledge.

You need the fretboard roadmaps if...

- ▶ All your soloing sounds the same and you want some different styles and flavors from which to choose.

- ▶ Some keys are harder to play in than others.

- ▶ Your guitar fretboard beyond the 5th fret is mysterious, uncharted territory.

- ▶ You can't automatically play any jazz lick you can think or hum.

- ▶ You can only learn a new tune by memorizing the chords, and you don't really understand the chord progression.

- ▶ You know a lot of "bits and pieces" on the guitar, but you don't have a system that ties it all together.

Read on, and many mysteries will be explained. If you're serious about playing jazz, the pages that follow can shed light and save you a great deal of time.

Good luck,

Fred Sokolow

> **This book is a jazz guitarist's extension of Fred Sokolow's *Fretboard Roadmaps*** (Hal Leonard Corporation, HL00696514), which includes even more music theory for guitarists, along with musical examples, solos and licks. We urge you to use *Fretboard Roadmaps* as a reference, along with *Fretboard Roadmaps for the Jazz Guitarist*.

THE RECORDING AND THE PRACTICE TRACKS

All the licks, riffs and tunes in this book are played on the accompanying CD.

There are also five practice tracks on the recording. Each one has a standard jazz groove and progression. They are mixed so that the lead guitar is on one side of your stereo and the backup band is on the other.

Each track contains a standard progression and illustrates the use of certain scales, chords, techniques or licks.

You can also tune out the lead guitar track and use the backup tracks to practice playing solos.

NOTES ON THE FRETBOARD
TIPS ON HOW TO LEARN THEM

#1

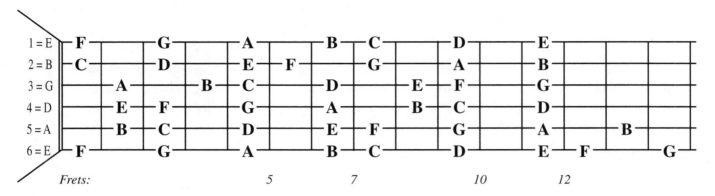

1 = E	F		G		A		B	C		D		E			
2 = B	C		D		E	F		G		A		B			
3 = G		A		B	C		D		E	F		G			
4 = D		E	F		G		A		B	C		D			
5 = A		B	C		D		E	F		G		A		B	
6 = E	F		G		A		B	C		D		E	F		G

Frets: 5   7   10   12

WHY?

▶ Knowing where the notes are (especially the notes on the 6th and 5th strings) will help you find chords and scales up and down the neck. It will help you alter and understand chords (e.g., *How do I flat the seventh in this chord? Why is this chord minor instead of major?*). It's a first step toward understanding music.

WHAT?

▶ *The notes get higher in pitch as you go up the alphabet and up the fretboard.*

▶ *A whole step is two frets, and a half step is one fret.*

▶ *Sharps are one fret higher:* 6th string/3rd fret = G, so 6th string/4th fret = G♯. 6th string/8th fret = C, so 6th string/9th fret = C♯.

▶ *Flats are one fret lower:* 6th string/5th fret = A, so 6th string/4th fret = A♭; 6th string/10th fret = D, so 6th string/9th fret = D♭.

HOW?

▶ *Fretboard markings help.* Most guitars have fretboard inlays or marks somewhere on the neck indicating the 5th, 7th, 10th and 12th frets. Become aware of these signposts.

DO IT!

▶ *Start by memorizing the notes on the 6th and 5th strings.* You will need to know these notes very soon–for Roadmap #3.

SUMMING UP—NOW YOU KNOW...

▶ *The location of the notes on the fretboard*

▶ *The meaning of these musical terms:*

whole step, half step, sharp (♯), flat (♭)

THE MAJOR SCALE

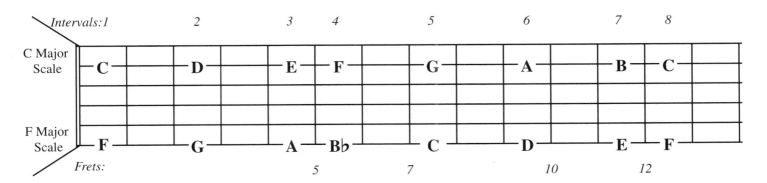

WHY?

▶ To understand music and to communicate with other players, you need to know about the major scale. The major scale is a ruler that helps you measure distances between notes and chords. Knowing the major scale will help you understand and talk about chord construction, scales and chord relationships.

WHAT?

▶ *The major scale is the "Do-Re-Mi" scale you have heard all your life.* Countless familiar tunes are composed of notes from this scale.

▶ *Intervals are distances between notes.* The intervals of the major scale are used to describe these distances. For example, E is the third note of the C major scale, and it is four frets above C (see above). This distance is called a *third*. Similarly, A is a third above F, and C♯ is a third above A. On the guitar, *a third is always a distance of four frets.*

HOW?

▶ *Every major scale has the same interval pattern of whole and half-steps:*

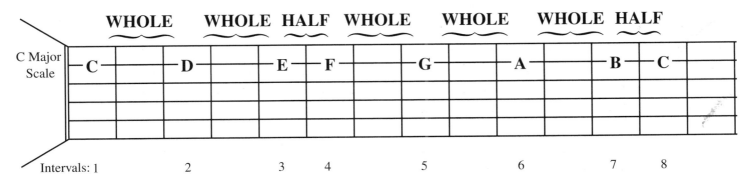

In other words, the major scale ascends and descends by whole steps (two frets at a time) with two exceptions: there is a half step (one fret) from the third to the fourth notes and from the seventh to the eighth notes. It's helpful to think of intervals in terms of frets (e.g., a third is 4 frets).

▶ *Intervals can extend above the octave.** They correspond to lower intervals: a 2nd above the octave is called a *9th,* a 4th above the octave is an *11th,* and so on:

C Major Scale

Intervals:

1	2	3	4	5	6	7	8	9	10	11	12	13

C	D	E	F	G	A	B	C	D	E	F	G	A

Frets: 5 7 10 12 15 17 20

DO IT!

▶ *Learn the major scale intervals* on one string by playing any note and finding the note that is a second (two frets) higher, a third (four frets) higher, and so on:

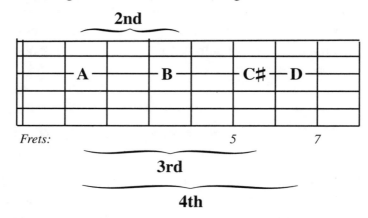

 ▶ Learn the sound of intervals by playing harmonies on two strings, as shown below. These moveable interval patterns will help you hear the sound of a third, a fourth and other intervals, if you play them all over the fretboard.

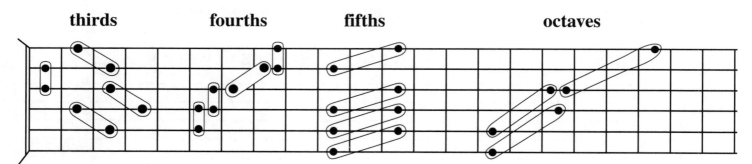

thirds   fourths   fifths   octaves

In each of the above pairs of notes, the higher note is a third, fourth, fifth or octave (as indicated) above the lower note.

SUMMING UP—NOW YOU KNOW...

▶ *The intervals of the major scale and the number of frets that make up each interval*

▶ *How to play thirds, fourths, fifths and octaves on two strings*

▶ *The meaning of the musical term "octave"*

* An "octave" is the interval between the 1st and 8th note of a major scale. An octave above C is a higher C note.

TWO MOVEABLE MAJOR CHORDS AND THEIR VARIATIONS

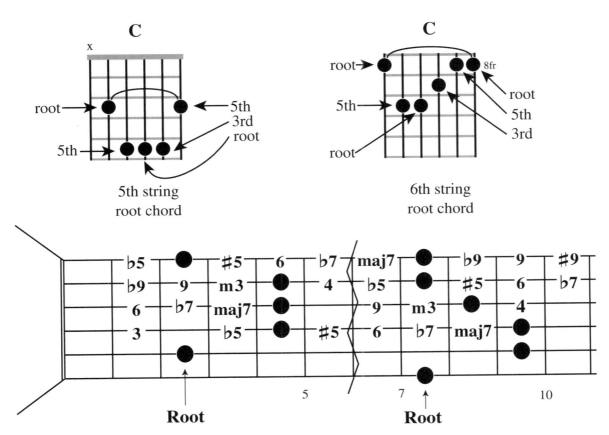

WHY?

► Jazz uses more chords than any other popular music. This roadmap helps build and expand your chord vocabulary. Moveable chords have no open (unfretted) strings, so they can be played (moved) all over the fretboard. **ROADMAP #3** shows how to play two moveable major chords and how to alter them slightly to create dozens of moveable jazz chord shapes.

WHAT?

► *A "chord" is a group of three or more notes played simultaneously.*

► *A "moveable chord" can be played all over the fretboard. It contains no open (unfretted) strings.*

► *A "root" is the note that gives a chord its name.*

► *All major chords consist of a root, 3rd and 5th.* Make sure you know the intervals in the moveable major chords of Roadmap #3. They are identified by the numbers with arrows on the chord grids.

► *You can create jazz chords (6ths, major 7ths, etc.) by adding or changing one note of a major chord.*

HOW?

▶ ***The 6th string identifies the 6th-string root/barred E chord.*** It's a G chord when played at the 3rd fret, because the 6th string/3rd fret is G. At the 6th fret it's a B♭ chord, and so on.

▶ ***The 5th string identifies the 5th-string root/barred A chord.*** It's a C chord at the 3rd fret, because the 5th string/3rd fret is C. At the 9th fret it's F♯ (G♭), and so on.

▶ Compare every new chord you learn to a basic chord you already know. Every small chord grid in the "DO IT" section, below, is a variation of a basic chord formation.

DO IT!

▶ ***Here are some variations of the two moveable major chords.*** Play them and compare each chord shape to the larger grid to the left, from which it is derived.

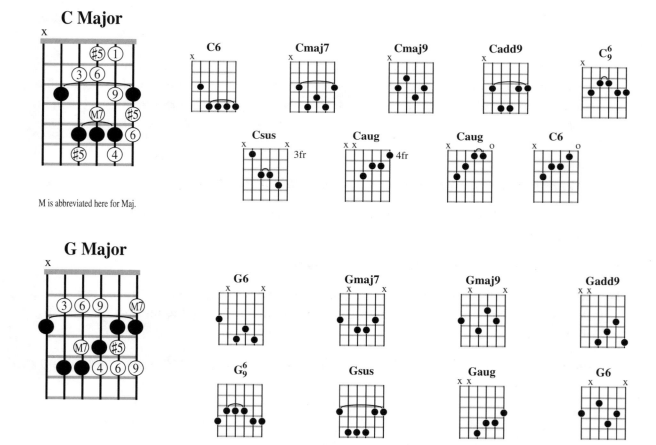

► *Flatting the 3rd in a major chord makes it minor.* Here are the moveable 6th string root and 5th string root minor chords and their variations:

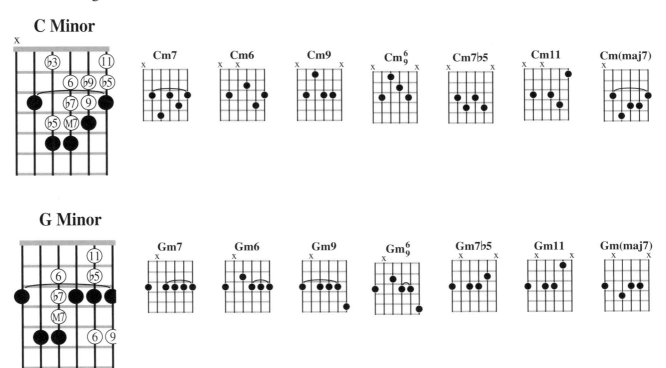

► Adding a flatted 7th to a major chord makes it a 7th (also called a dominant 7th) chord. Here are the moveable 6th-string root and 5th-string root 7th chords and their variations:

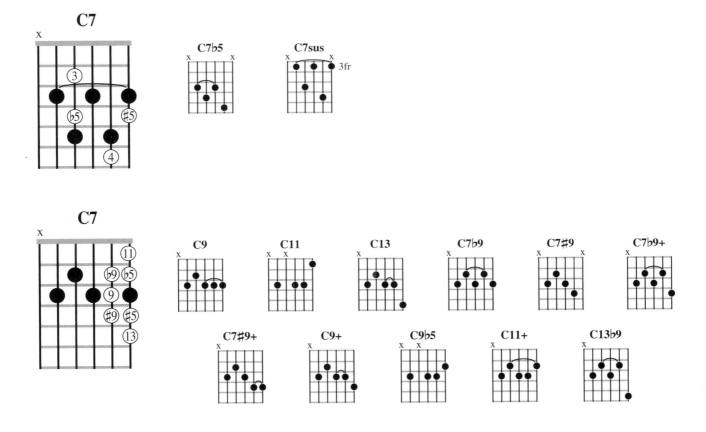

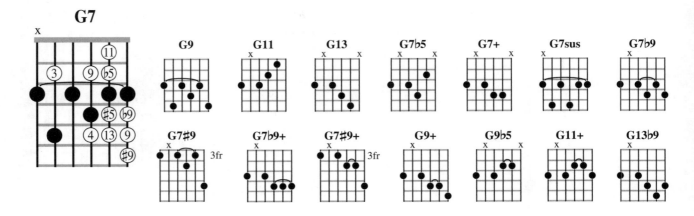

► *Flatting the 3rd, 5th and ♭7th of a 7th chord makes it a diminished chord.* Here are the moveable 6th-string root and 5th-string root diminished chords:

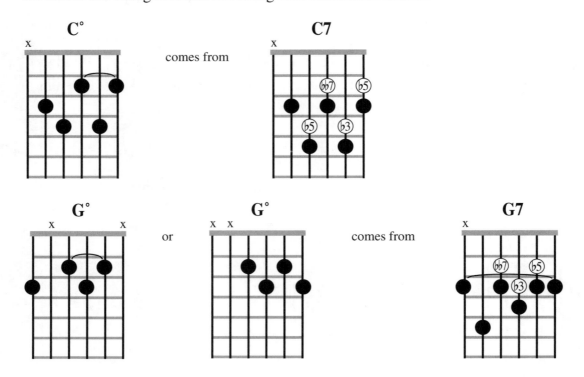

Diminished chords repeat every three frets, so you can play any diminished chord several ways:

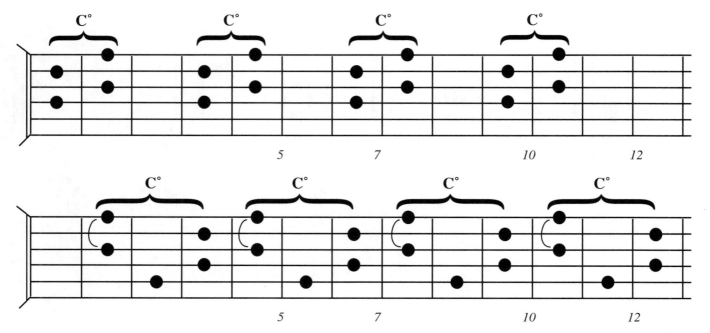

▶ *Raising the 5th of a major chord makes it an augmented chord.* Here are the moveable 6th string root and 5th string root augmented chords:

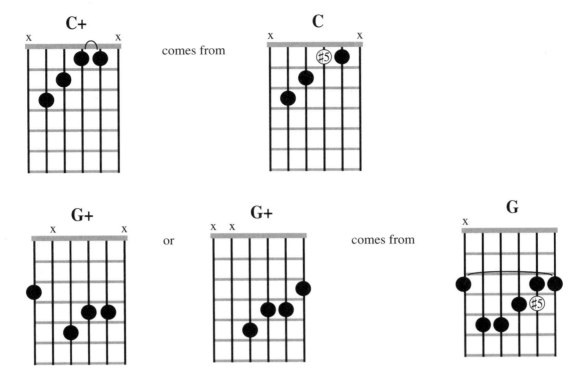

Augmented chords repeat every four frets, so you can play any augmented chord several ways:

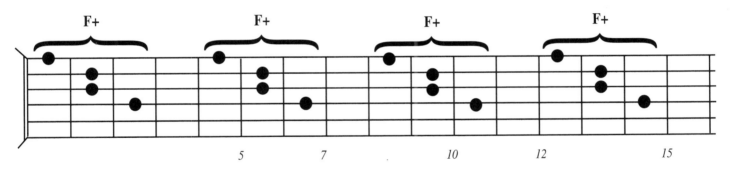

▶ *Learn the sound of each chord type (9th, 13th, major 7) by playing each "type" all over the fretboard, with a 5th and 6th string root:*

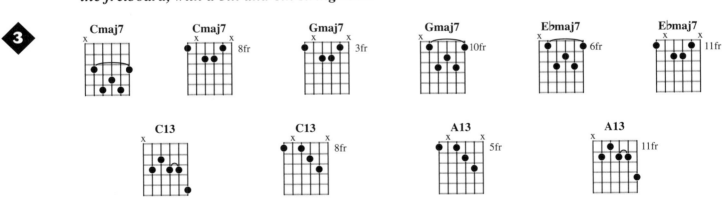

SUMMING UP—NOW YOU KNOW...

▶ *The intervals that make up a major chord* (the 1st, 3rd and 5th)

▶ *How to play any major chord two ways:* Using a moveable chord with a 6th string root and a moveable chord with a 5th string root

▶ *Five types of chords (major, minor, 7th, diminished and augmented) and how to play many variations of each type,* with a 5th and 6th string root

▶ *The meaning of these musical terms:*

Chord, moveable chord, root, major, minor, seventh, diminished, augmented

I–IV–V CHORD FAMILIES, SIMPLE PROGRESSIONS

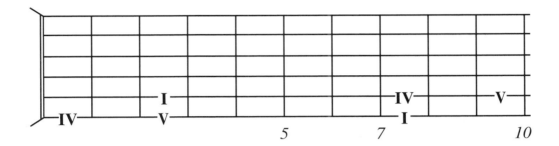

WHY?

▶ The *I–IV–V chord family* is the basis for countless chord progressions. This roadmap shows you how to locate chord families automatically in any key, all over the fretboard.

WHAT?

▶ *The Roman numerals in the chart above are the roots of the I, IV and V chords in the key of C.*

▶ *The numbers I, IV and V refer to the major scale of your key.* F is the fourth note in the C major scale, so an F chord is the IV chord in the key of C.

HOW?

▶ *The I-IV-V root patterns in the fretboard chart are moveable.*

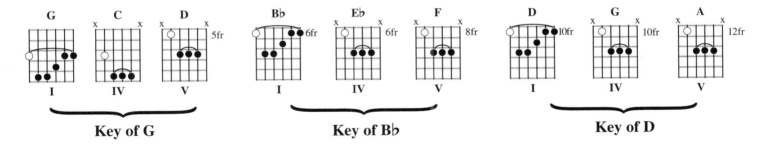

▶ *Variations of the two moveable major chords can be used in the chord family.* Whether you play 6ths, 7ths, major 7ths, etc., the I–IV–V root relationships are the same.

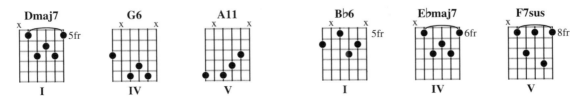

DO IT!

► *Play these common I–IV–V progressions.* Use these three steps on each sample progression:

▷ Play it as it's written (read the ink!)

▷ Play it in other keys (move it up the fretboard)

▷ If it is written with a 6th string root I chord, play it with a 5th string root I chord, and vice versa.

Each bar has four beats. The repeat sign ⁄⁄ means "repeat the previous bar."

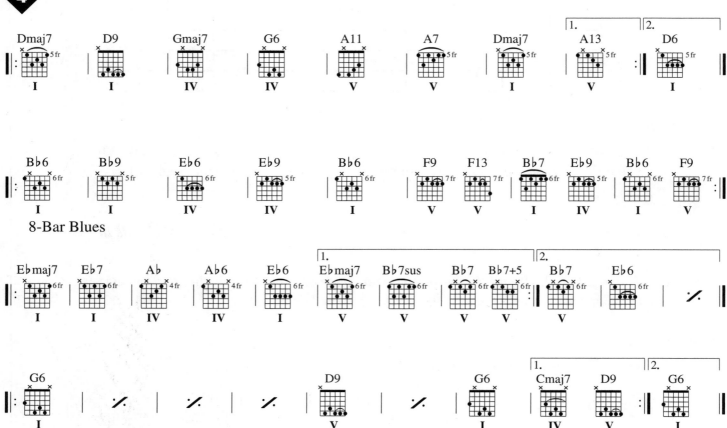

8-Bar Blues

► *Play the 12-bar blues progression in several keys:* It's the basis of countless jazz, blues and rock tunes, such as "Bag's Groove," "Billie's Bounce," "Route 66," "Stormy Monday," "Hound Dog," "Johnny B. Goode," "Blue Monk," "Kansas City," "Au Privave," "C Jam Blues," "Fine and Mellow" and "Shake, Rattle and Roll." Here it is (with no frills—there are many variations) in A:

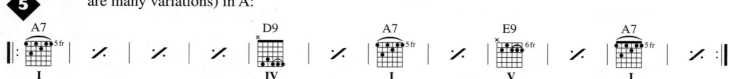

Use the following chord families to play the blues progression in different keys, humming the tunes mentioned above while strumming the chords:

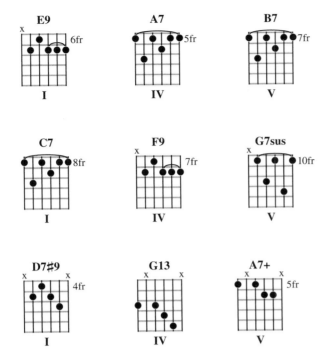

SUMMING UP—NOW YOU KNOW...

▶ *Two different ways to play the I–IV–V chord family—in any key:* with a 6th string root/I chord and with a 5th string root/I chord

▶ *How to play the 12-bar blues and many I–IV–V progressions in any key, two ways*

▶ *How to use many chord variations within the I–IV–V chord families*

▶ *The meaning of these musical terms:*

I chord, IV chord, V chord, 12-Bar Blues

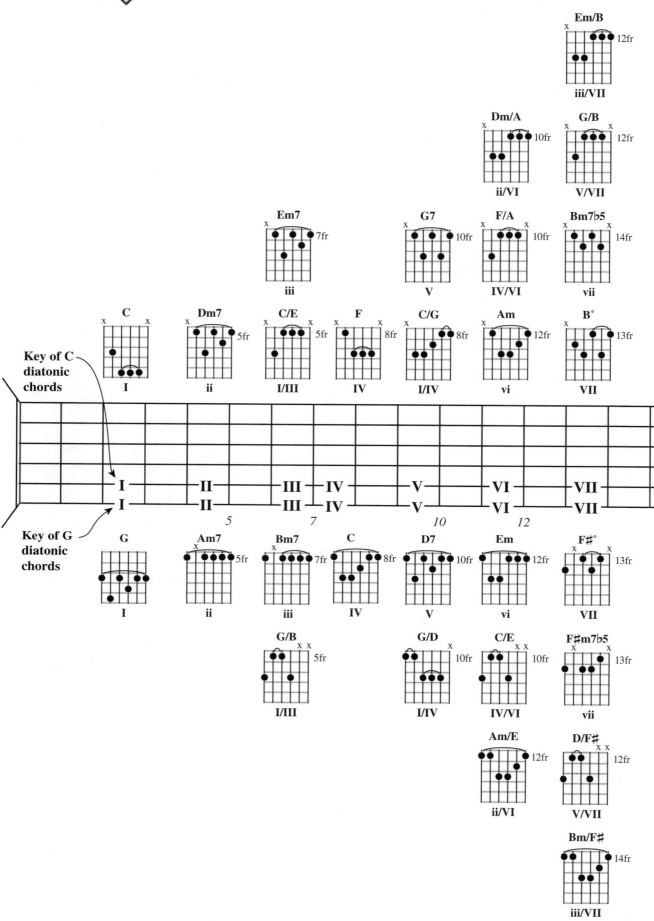

WHY?

► Many songs are based on (or include) scalewise movement. If you understand this type of progression as well as circle of fifths movement (the subject of the next chapter) and I–IV–V (blues and folk) chord changes, you can grasp nearly any jazz or pop song. **ROADMAP #5** shows how to "automatically" play scalewise progressions.

WHAT?

► *Many progressions consist of ascending or descending chords.* **ROADMAP #5** shows two ascending progressions—one in C and one in G.

► *The roots of the chords go up or down the major scale of your key.* If you're in the key of G, you go up or down the G scale, playing a chord with each ascending or descending note. Each chord harmonizes with your key, because it's *diatonic*—it's composed of notes from the major scale of the song's key.

HOW?

► *Here are the diatonic chords* (as shown in **ROADMAP #5**) for the key of C. As you can see, there are sometimes several choices for a given scale degree:

The 2nd scale degree is a minor chord (Dm).
The 3rd scale degree is minor (Em) or a I chord with the IIIrd in the bass (C/E).
The 4th scale degree is a major chord (F).
The 5th scale degree is a major chord (G or G7) or I/V (C/G).
The 6th scale degree is a minor chord (Am) or IV/VI (F/A) or ii/VI (Dm/A).
The 7th scale degree is a diminished chord (B°) or m7♭5 (Bm7♭5) or V/VII (G/B) or iii/VII (Em/B).

► *You can substitute chords of the same letter-name and same "type" (major or minor).* C can be C6 or Cmaj7, Am can be Am9, Am7, etc.

► *You can play diminished chords between scale degrees,* especially between the 1st and 2nd and 3rd degrees (ascending) and between the 3rd and 2nd degrees (descending):

Key of C

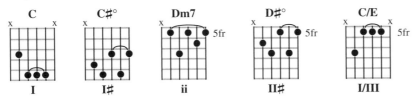

Key of G

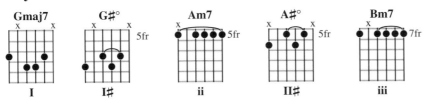

DO IT!

► *Play these scalewise progressions in different keys:*

Key of G

Gmaj7	Am7	Bm7	Cmaj7	D9		Em7		F#m7b5	B7	‖ Cmaj7	G/B		Am7	Gmaj7	‖
I	ii	iii	IV	V		vi		vii		IV	I/III		ii	I	

Key of C

Cmaj7	Dm7	C/E	Fmaj7	Em7		Dm7	Cmaj7		Bm7b5	Am7		E7		Am7	‖
I	ii	I/III	IV	iii		ii	I		vii	vi					

► *Play these scalewise progressions; they include diminished chords between scale degrees:*

Key of G

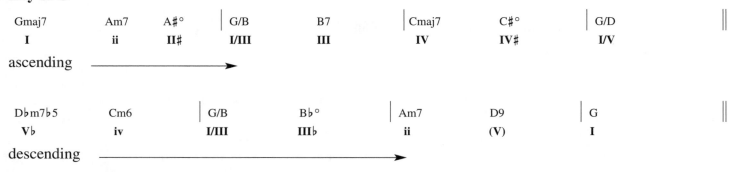

Gmaj7		Am7	A#°		G/B		B7		Cmaj7		C#°		G/D		‖
I		ii	II#		I/III		III		IV		IV#		I/V		

ascending ⟶

Dbm7b5		Cm6		G/B		Bb°		Am7		D9		G		‖
Vb		iv		I/III		IIIb		ii		(V)		I		

descending ⟶

► *In many songs, scalewise progressions are mixed with other types of chord movement.* The following 8-bar phrase is the basis for many standards, including (with some variations) "Ain't Misbehavin'," "Tiptoe Through theTulips," "The Glory of Love," "The Birth of the Blues" and "Makin' Whoopee." The first half is mostly a scalewise ascent. The next four bars consist of circle of fifths movement and a turnaround, both of which are explained in the next chapter.

Key of G

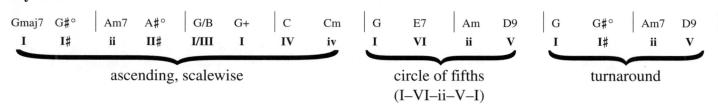

Gmaj7	G#°	Am7	A#°	G/B	G+	C	Cm	G	E7	Am	D9	G	G#°	Am7	D9	‖
I	I#	ii	II#	I/III	I	IV	iv	I	VI	ii	V	I	I#	ii	V	

ascending, scalewise   circle of fifths (I–VI–ii–V–I)   turnaround

► *While comping (playing chord backup), jazz guitarists often embellish chord progressions with scalewise chord substitutions.* Four bars of I chord can become:

Key of G, ascending and descending   or

G	G/B	C	C#°	G/D	G/B	Bb°	Am7	‖ G	G#°	Am7	A#°	Bm7	A#°	Am7	G	‖
I	I/III	IV	IV#	I/V	I/III	II#	ii	I	I#	ii	II#	iii	II#	ii	I	

Here's a 12-bar blues, made fancier with scalewise movement:

Key of B♭

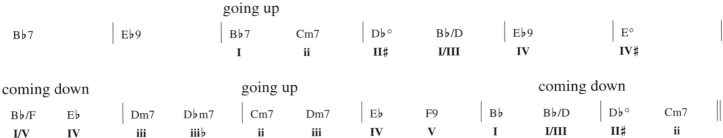

		going up				
B♭7	E♭9	B♭7 Cm7	D♭° B♭/D	E♭9	E°	
		I ii	II♯ I/III	IV	IV♯	

coming down			going up			coming down	
B♭/F E♭	Dm7 D♭m7	Cm7 Dm7	E♭ F9	B♭ B♭/D	D♭° Cm7
I/V IV	iii iiib	ii iii	IV V	I I/III	II♯ ii

Many popular songs have a 32-bar, AABA format. "Once around the tune" consists of:

▷ an 8 bar phrase (A)

▷ a repeat of the A part

▷ a different 8 bar phrase, called a bridge (B)

▷ Another repeat of A

The "Honeysuckle Rose" bridge is used in countless standards besides the song that gave it that name, including "Satin Doll," "On the Sunny Side of the Street," "I'm Confessing," "September in the Rain," "I Don't Want to Set the World On Fire" and "The Object of my Affection." Here it is, in its simplest form:

Key of G

G7	℅	C	℅	A7	℅	D7	℅	
I		IV		II		V		

Here's the "Honeysuckle Rose" bridge, embellished with scalewise movement:

G7 Am7	A♯° G/B	C Dm7	D♭° C/E	A7 G/B	C° A/C♯	D7 C/E	F° D/F♯	
I ii	II♯ I/III	I ii	II♯ I/III	V IV/VI	VI♯ V/VII	V IV/VI	VI♯ V/VII	

key changes: key of C   key of D   key of G

SUMMING UP—NOW YOU KNOW...

▶ *How to play scalewise chord progressions*

▶ *How to play diminished chords between scale degrees*

▶ *How to embellish simple progressions with scalewise movement*

▶ *A standard "Ain't Misbehavin'"-style 8 bar/scalewise progression*

▶ *The AABA format of many popular songs*

▶ *How to play and embellish the "Honeysuckle Rose" bridge,* and the meaning of the musical term "bridge"

CIRCLE OF FIFTHS PROGRESSION

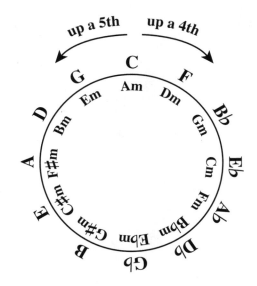

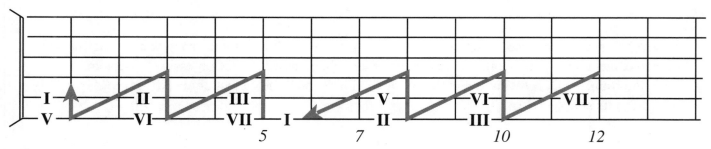

WHY?

▶ Countless jazz standards include (or consist mainly of) circle of fifths movement. It's easy to learn songs and comprehend chord progressions once you understand these "standard changes."

WHAT?

▶ The circle of fifths (also called the "circle of fourths") arranges the twelve musical notes so that *a step counter-clockwise takes you up a fifth, and a step clockwise takes you up a fourth.*

▷ Counter-clockwise: G is a fifth above C, B a fifth above E, etc.

▷ Clockwise: F is a fourth above C, B♭ is a fourth above F, etc.

HOW?

▶ *In circle-of-fifths progressions, you leave the I chord (creating tension) and come back to I (resolving tension) by clockwise motion,* going up by fourths until you are "home" at the I chord. For example, in the key of C:

Notice the second chord (A7) takes you away from C and the key-of-C chord family, and you get back to C by going clockwise along the circle: Dm is a fourth above A, G7 is a fourth above Dm and C is a fourth above G7.

▶ *As you move clockwise along the circle, the chords can be major or minor,* but the V chord is almost always a dominant 7th.

▶ *The zig-zag motion shown in* **ROADMAP #6** *(starting at VII and ending at I) is circle of fifths motion.* Each Roman numeral is the root of a chord, and each zig or zag takes you to the chord that is a fourth higher, until you're home at the I chord. For example, in the key of C, you zig-zag "home" from the VI chord like this:

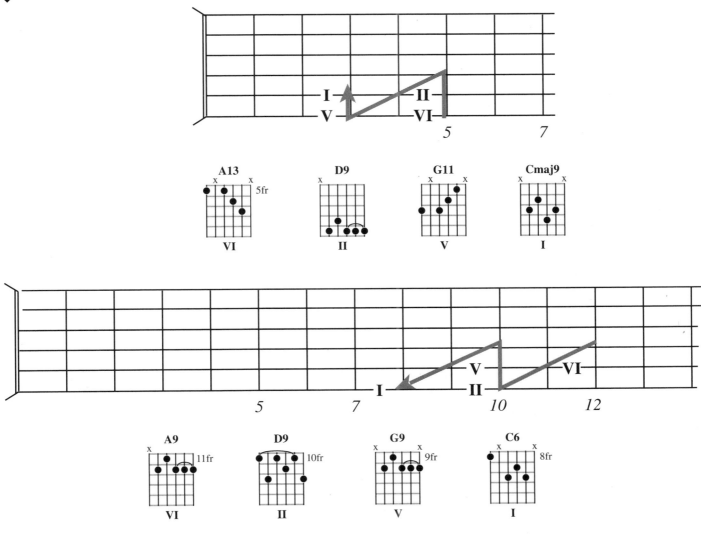

DO IT!

▶ *Play ii–V–I progressions in many keys, using a variety of jazz chords.* Notice the zig-zag motion of the roots of chords, as you play them:

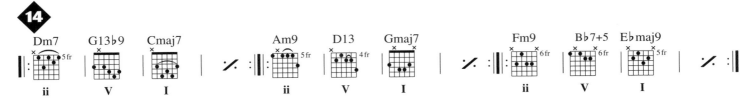

▶ ***Do the same with I–vi–ii–V.*** This progression is so common that pros have nicknamed it "standard changes," "dimestore progression," "ice cream changes," "I Got Rhythm changes," etc. It's the basis for countless standards ("Blue Moon," "Heart and Soul," "These Foolish Things," "I Got Rhythm," "More") and "classic rock" tunes ("Oh Donna," "You Send Me," "Stand By Me," "Every Time You Go Away," "Every Breath You Take," "[Everybody Has a] Hungry Heart").

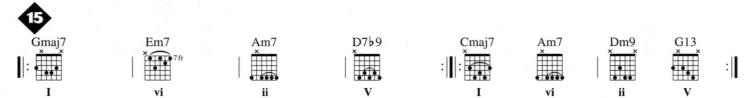

If you substitute I♯° (the diminished chord a fret above the I chord) for vi, the result is a popular progression or "turnaround"* used in countless tunes:

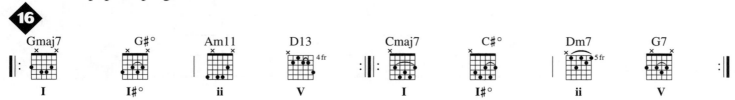

▶ Play the I–VI–II–V progression, where VI, II and V are 7th chords. Songs like "Sweet Georgia Brown," "Deep Purple," "Up the Lazy River" and "I Ain't Got Nobody" begin with a "walk down" to VI from I:

The descending I chord is your clue that a VI–II–V–I progression is in progress.

▶ ***Jazz players often "cycle back" to a VI–II–V–I progression to extend a tune's ending.*** Instead of resolving the final V chord with I, they go to the VI and come back along the circle:

Key of F:

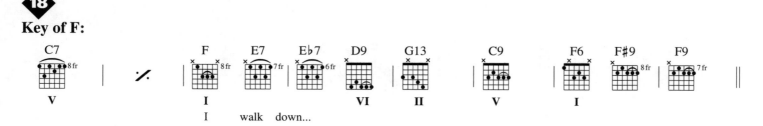

▶ ***Play III–VI–II–V–I progressions.*** This goes a step farther back on the circle than VI-II-V-I. It's the "I Got Rhythm Bridge" that is used in so many tunes ("Side by Side,"

*A "turnaround" is a short (usually 2-bar) phrase at the end of a chorus that sets up a repeat of the chorus.

"Straighten Up and Fly Right," "Sunday," "Please Don't Talk About Me When I'm Gone"), and if you begin with a I chord it's the basis for "All of Me," "Who's Sorry Now" and many standards.

19

"I Got Rhythm" bridge, key of G:

B7	./.	E9	./.	A7	./.	D9	./.	G	
III		VI		II		V		I etc.	

Another III–VI–II–I Progression:

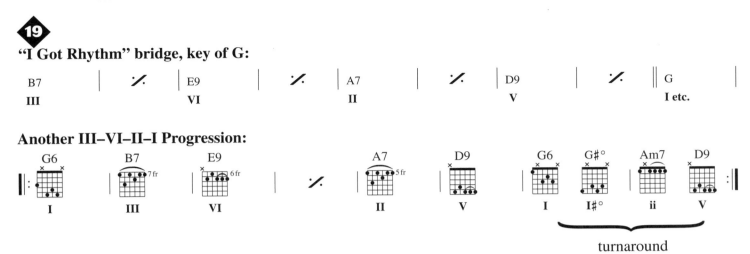

turnaround

Sometimes the III, VI or II are minor, in a III–VI–II–V–I progression:

20

Key of F: **Key of B♭**

Am7	Dm7	Gm7	C9	Fmaj7	Dm7	G7♭9	Cm7	F7♭9	B♭maj7	
iii	vi	ii	V	I	iii	VI	ii	V	I	

▶ While "cycling back to I" from III or from VI, you can play substitutions for every other chord, creating a chromatic (one-fret-at-a- time) descent. The substitute chords are a flatted fifth below the actual chord (e.g. if the given chord is E7, B♭7 is substituted). Here are some samples:

21

Key of F: **Key of B♭**

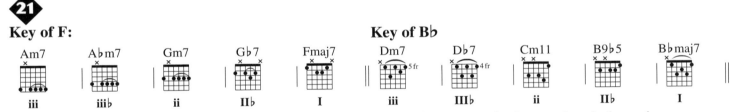

Am7	A♭m7	Gm7	G♭7	Fmaj7	Dm7	D♭7	Cm11	B9♭5	B♭maj7	
iii	iii♭	ii	II♭	I	iii	III♭	ii	II♭	I	

▶ *Play VII–III–VI–II–V–I progressions,* cycling back one step farther on the circle, as in "Mister Sandman" and "Red Roses for a Blue Lady."

22

Key of C:

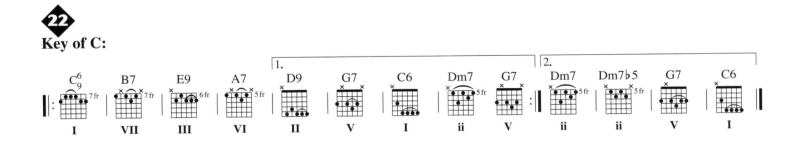

C⁶/₉	B7	E9	A7	**1.** D9	G7	C6	Dm7	G7	**2.** Dm7	Dm7♭5	G7	C6
I	VII	III	VI	II	V	I	ii	V	ii	ii	V	I

► *You can make simple chord progressions fancier by adding circle of fifths motion.* This uptown version of a 12-bar blues in B♭ includes circle of fifths chord movement with chromatic (♭5) substitutions:

Key of G:

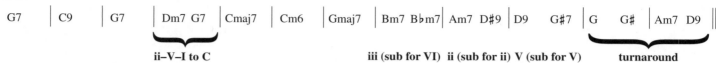

| G7 | C9 | G7 | Dm7 G7 | Cmaj7 | Cm6 | Gmaj7 | Bm7 B♭m7 | Am7 D♯9 | D9 G♯7 | G G♯ | Am7 D9 |

                   ii–V–I to C   iii (sub for VI) ii (sub for ii) V (sub for V)   turnaround

► Many songs combine I–IV–V and circle of fifths changes, like the following 8-bar tune:

Key of C:

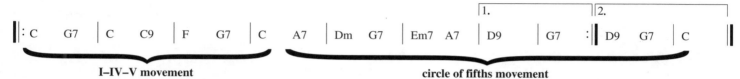

| ‖: C G7 | C C9 | F G7 | C A7 | Dm G7 | Em7 A7 | ¹·D9 | G7 :‖ ²·D9 G7 | C ‖ |

               I–IV–V movement   circle of fifths movement

The following 8-bar phrase ends many a 32-bar tune, including "All Of Me," "Sit Right Down and Write Myself a Letter," "Pennies From Heaven," "Paper Doll," "On a Slow Boat to China," "Who's Sorry Now," "Mona Lisa," "It's a Sin to Tell a Lie" and "But Not For Me." It combines I-IV-V and circle of fifths changes:

Key of C:

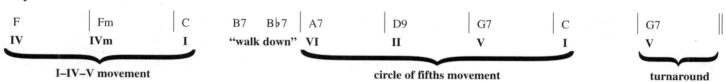

F	Fm	C	B7 B♭7	A7	D9	G7	C	G7 ‖
IV	IVm	I	"walk down" VI		II	V	I	V

         I–IV–V movement   circle of fifths movement   turnaround

The "Honeysuckle Rose" bridge, mentioned in the previous chapter, can be understood in circle of fifths terms, especially when a few minor chords are added to the basic progression:

Key of F:

| Cm7 | F7 | B♭ | ∕· | Dm7 | G7 | C7 | ∕· ‖ |

        ii–V–I to the B♭ (IV chord)   vi   –   II   –   V

SUMMING UP—NOW YOU KNOW...

► *How to play several circle of fifths progressions in any key* using the "zig-zag" method

► *Several standard chord progressions,* including the "I Got Rhythm" bridge

► *The meaning of the musical term "turnaround"* and how to play one

► *How to play ♭5 substitutions during circle of fifths movement*

► *How to embellish a 12-bar blues with circle-of-fifths movement*

THE F–D–A ROADMAP

All F Chords:

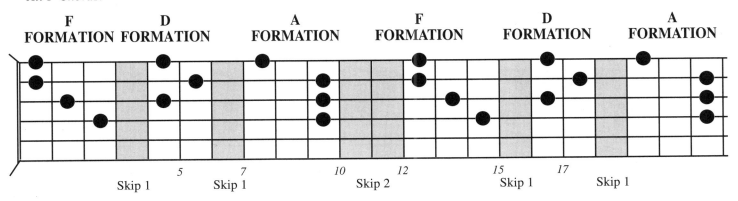

WHY?

► **ROADMAP #7** gives you chord choices. It shows you how to play any chord in a high, low or middle register on the fretboard, automatically. It enriches your comping (backup) and it's essential for chord-melody playing, or chord-based soloing.

WHAT?

► The chords on **ROADMAP #7** are all F chords. Because they are abbreviated, 3- or 4-note chord formations, they are sometimes called *chord fragments.*

HOW?

► *To memorize this roadmap,* remember: *F-SKIP 1, D-SKIP 1, A-SKIP 2.* In other words, play an F formation, skip a fret, play a D formation, skip a fret, play an A formation, skip two frets.

► *You can climb the fretboard starting with any chord formation.* The F–D–A roadmap is a continuous loop that you can enter at any point. It can be the D–A–F or A–F–D roadmap. The "skips" are always the same: one skip after F, one after D, two after A. Here are all the D chords:

All D Chords:

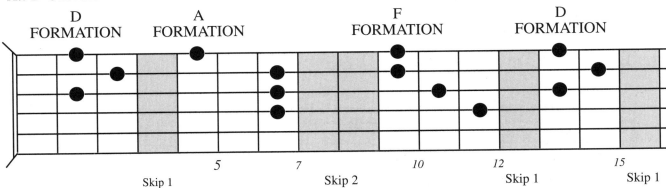

► **You can make the major chord fragments into 7ths or minors.** This creates new roadmaps that give you more chord versatility:

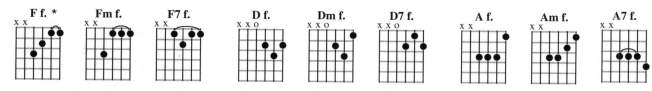

All Fm Chords:

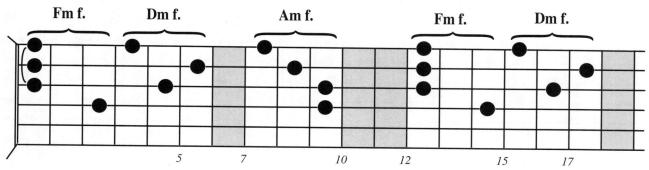

All F7 Chords:

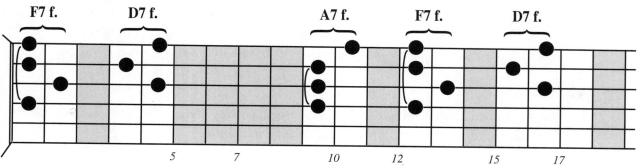

DO IT!

► *Practice climbing the fretboard with 7th and minor chords:*

All C7 Chords:

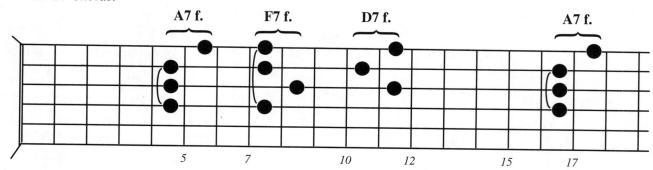

All B♭m Chords:

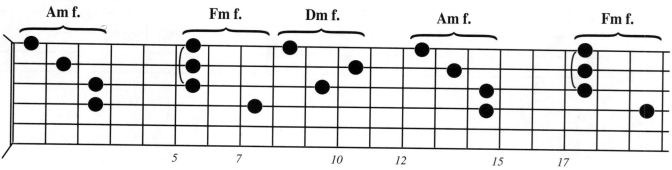

Note: f. is the abbreviation for formation.

▶ Use the F–D–A roadmap for chord solos whenever a tune stays on one chord for several bars. For example, in the "I Got Rhythm" bridge in B♭:

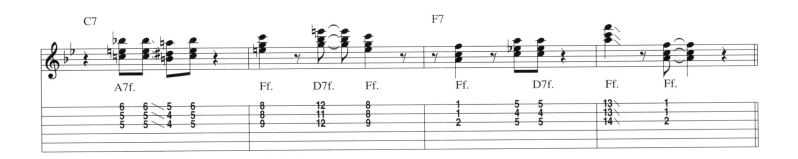

▶ Play solos and licks by "arpeggiating" chord fragments. Playing an arpeggio is picking the notes of a chord in succession, going up or down the strings in a harp-like fashion:

Here's the previous 8-bar bridge, spiced up with arpeggios.

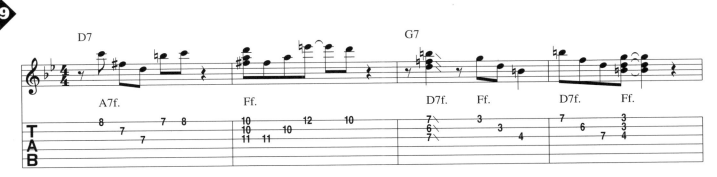

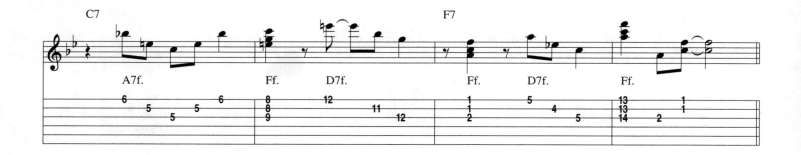

SUMMING UP—NOW YOU KNOW...

▶ *How to play three major chord fragments*

▶ *How to change them into minor and 7th chord fragements*

▶ *How to use them to play any major, minor or 7th chord all over the fretboard* (with the F–D–A roadmap)

▶ *How to build solos by arpeggiating chord fragments*

CHORD-BASED SOLOING

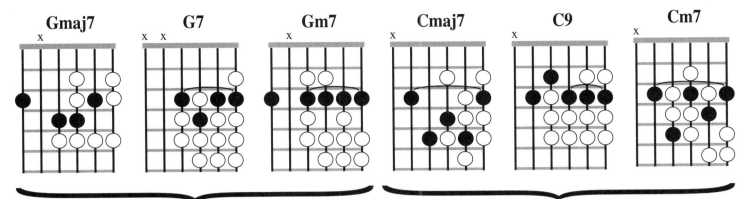

Gmaj7   G7   Gm7   Cmaj7   C9   Cm7

6th string root/chords   **5th string root/chords**

WHY?

▶ It's easy to vary a chord formation by adding or changing a note or two. These chord embell-ishments can be the basis for *licks* (musical phrases), and single-note solos or chord solos. In an ensemble, chord-based soloing is as useful to the jazz guitarist as scale-based solo-ing. It's even more important to the unaccompanied guitarist.

WHAT?

▶ *Each chord shape in Roadmap #8 is surrounded by circled notes, which can be played with the basic chord formation.* Sometimes you add a note with a spare fretting finger, some-times you change fingering to flat a note.

▶ *You can follow a song's chord progression and ad-lib solos* by playing licks that are based on these chord embellishments.

▶ *You can use the same embellishments to play chord-melody solos.* This is the tradition, as old as jazz guitar, of playing chords and melody at the same time, with the melody notes at the "top" (the highest note) of each chord.

▶ *Chord-based licks can consist of a string of single notes or harmonized notes.* The harmony comes from strumming or picking two or three strings of a chord.

HOW?

▶ *Play the following chord-based licks.* Keep your left hand loosely in the pictured chord posi-tion so that you can occasionally harmonize notes. Joe Pass used to say that he always had a chord position "in mind," even when playing single-note licks.

30

29

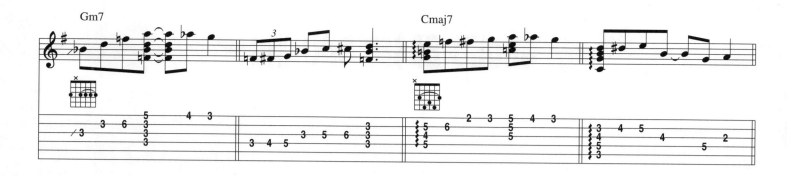

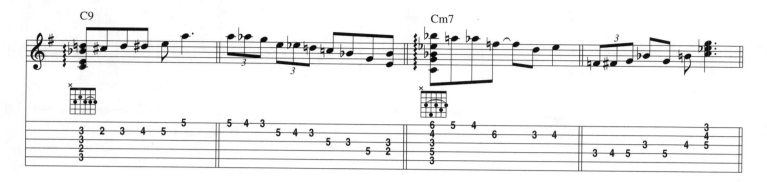

DO IT!

▶ Here are some chord-based solos for typical jazz progressions like ii–V–I and I–vi–ii–V.
Play them, then make up your own chord-based solos for the same progressions.

ii–V–I in G

ii–V–I in C

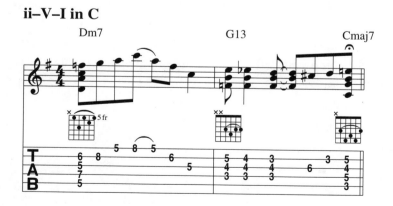

I–vi–ii–V in G

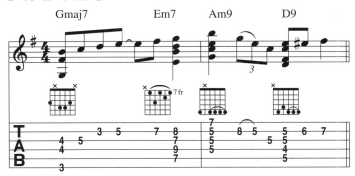

I–vi–ii–V in C

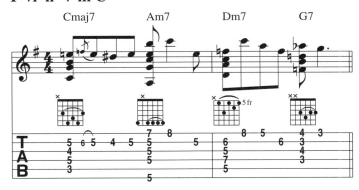

▶ *Practice playing similar passages in other keys.* Since the chord- based licks are moveable, key should make no difference.

▶ Play this chord-melody solo of the old standard, "Whispering." It's an example of using chords and chord-based licks to express a melody.

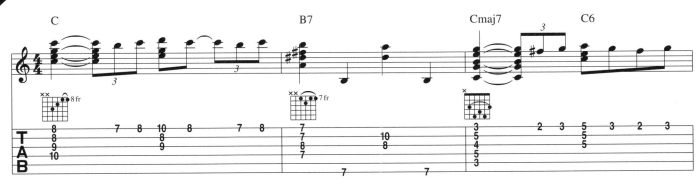

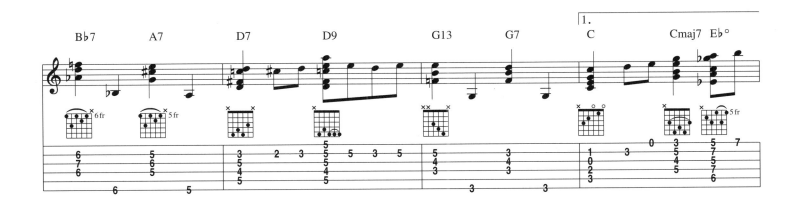

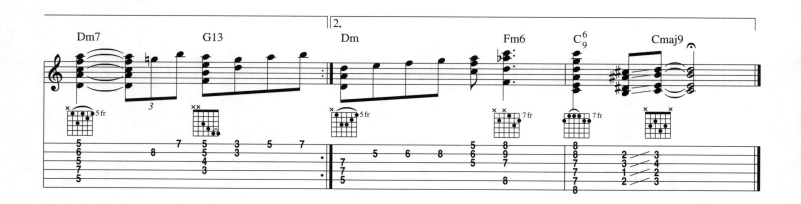

SUMMING UP—NOW YOU KNOW...

▶ *How to base licks and solos on moveable chord formations*

▶ *How to improvise, chord-style, over standard changes like ii–V–I or vi–ii–V–I*

▶ *How to play single-note and harmonized licks that are chord-based*

▶ *How to play a chord-melody solo using moveable chords and chord-based licks*

#9 MAJOR SCALES

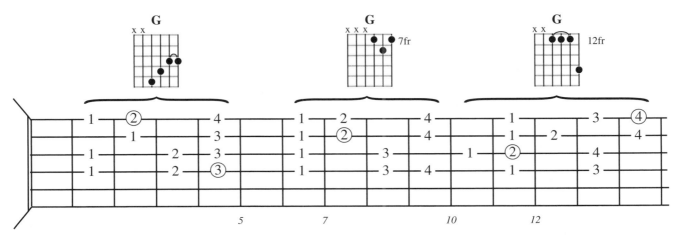

WHY?

► The major scale is the basis for countless melodies. Familiarity with moveable major scales allows you to play melodies and improvise solos. It brings you a step closer to any player's goal: to be able to *play* whatever you can hear.

WHAT?

► *Each of the three G major scales in Roadmap #9 is based on one of the three chord fragments* of **ROADMAP #7**. The root notes are circled. Play the appropriate chord fragment to get your fretting hand "in position" to play one of the major scales.

► The numbers on **ROADMAP #9** are left-hand fingering suggestions.

► **ROADMAP #9** *shows that there are three major scales for ANY chord.* To find the three D major scales, play all the D chords (using the F–D–A concept of **ROADMAP #7**). There's a D major scale for each D major chord fragment.

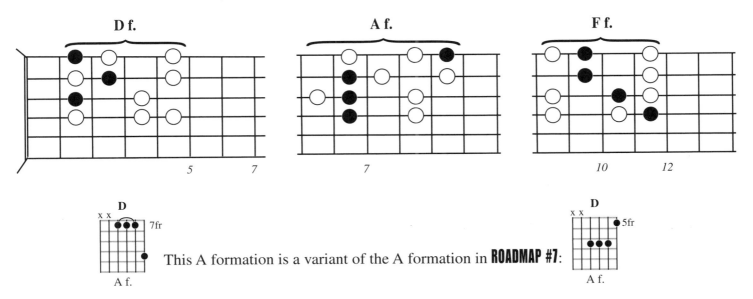

This A formation is a variant of the A formation in **ROADMAP #7**:

► *The major scale patterns can include all six strings,* which enables you to play melodies that include lower notes:

G Major Scales

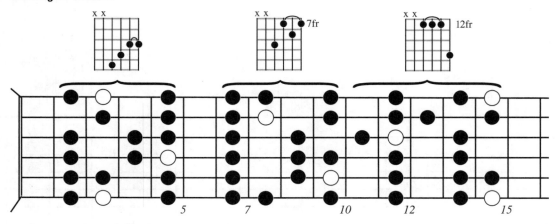

HOW?

► *Practice playing each moveable scale over and over* until it comes naturally. "Loop" them as shown below:

G Major Scale (F f.)

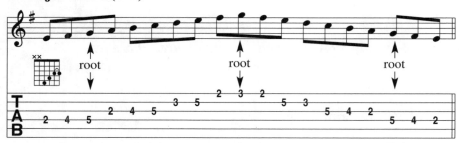
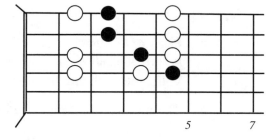

G Major Scale (D f.)

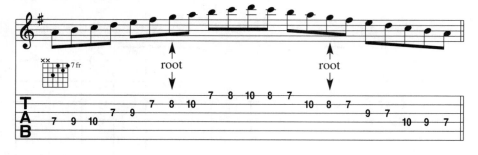
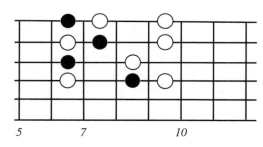

G Major Scale (A f.)

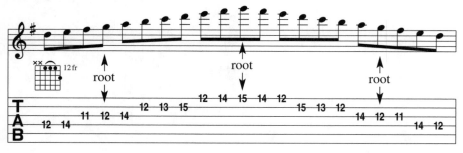
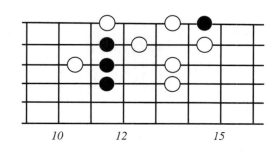

► *As long as a song stays in one key, you can ad lib solos based on the major scale of that key.*

► *When a song changes keys, use the major scale of the new key as a basis for soloing.* Although songs usually end in the key in which they begin, some songs have more than one "key center"; they *modulate* (change keys) a few times before returning to their original key. Many songs include a *bridge* (a middle section) in a key that differs from the rest of the tune.

The soloist needs to identify the key centers within a song and play the appropriate major scales. There are several examples in the "DO IT" section, below.

DO IT!

► *Use G major scales to solo on this I–vi–ii–V tune:*

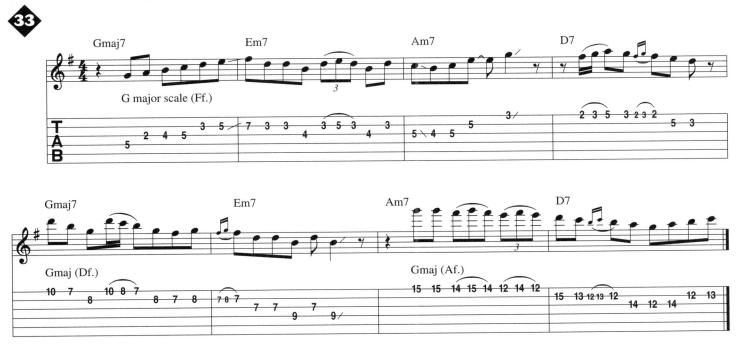

► *If a song includes chords that are not diatonic, switch from major-scale-based soloing to chord-based soloing* during those chords. The example below contains both types of soloing:

Chord-based licks

Fade

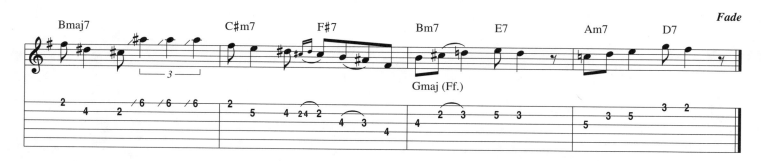

Gmaj (Ff.)

▶ *If a song has more than one key center, change major scales with the changing keys.* The following tune has the much-used AABA format (see **ROADMAP #5**). The A part is in the key of G. The bridge has a format found in many standards: it starts in the key of B (a 3rd higher than G) and modulates to D (a 5th above G), ending on a D7, which sets up a return to the key of G.* The soloist uses a G major scale during the A sections and switches to a B major scale, then a D major scale, for the bridge.

*A dominant 7th chord leads up a 4th: D7, for example, resolves to G. You can modulate to a new key by playing the dominant 7th chord that is a fifth above your destination key. (To get to the key of E♭, play B♭7.)

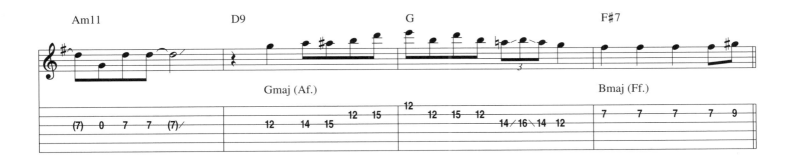

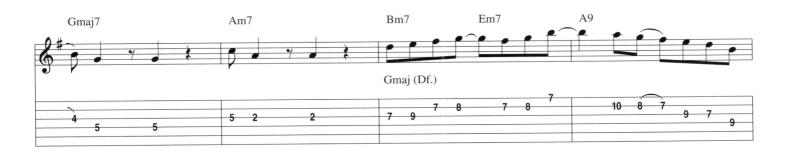

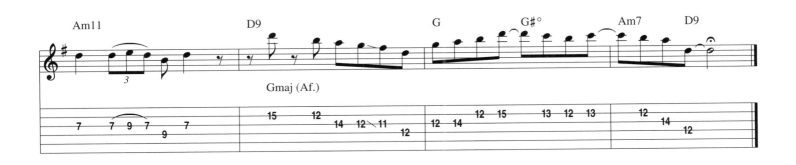

▶ *Play the melody to "Whispering" in C, using the C major scale.* (With the exception of two notes, the whole melody stays in the C major scale.) Then play it in other keys.

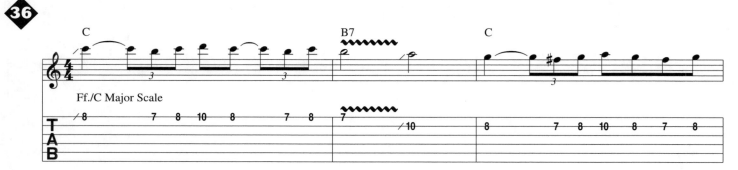

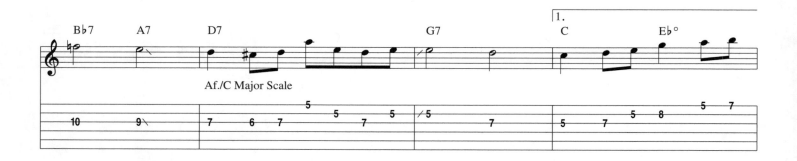

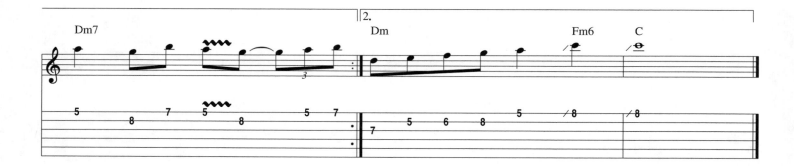

SUMMING UP—NOW YOU KNOW...

▶ *How to play three moveable major scales*

▶ *How to use them to ad lib solos or play melodies in any key*

▶ *How to identify key centers and change major scales to match them*

BLUES BOXES

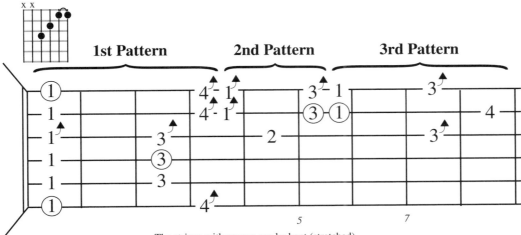

1st Pattern **2nd Pattern** **3rd Pattern**

The strings with arrows can be bent (stretched)

WHY?

▶ The blues is one of the foundations of jazz, and the blues boxes of **ROADMAP #10** are move-able scales that allow you to improvise bluesy solos and play blues melodies.

WHAT?

▶ *The three patterns in* **ROADMAP #10** *are F blues boxes.* The root notes are circled and the numbers are left-hand fingering suggestions.

▶ *The scale notes with arrows (- 4 -) can be stretched or choked.* Bending notes by stretch-ing strings is a fundamental part of the blues sound.

▶ *The blues scale is pentatonic;* it contains five notes: the 1st, ♭3rd, 4th, 5th and ♭7th. But other notes can be added, and the bottom-line rule for all music applies: whatever sounds right is right.

▶ *You can play the appropriate blues scale for a whole song,* or for long passages within a song.

HOW?

▶ *To get your left hand in position for the first blues box, play an F formation tonic chord.* For the key of G, play an F formation/G chord (at the 3rd fret) and play the scale and licks that follow (you don't have to maintain the F formation while playing the scale, but use it as a reference point):

G Blues—First Pattern

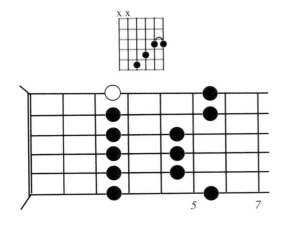

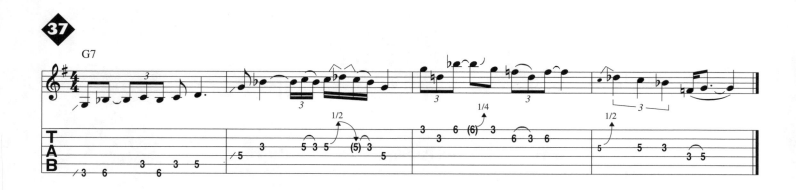

▶ *To get your left hand in position for the second blues box, slide up to the root note on the 2nd string with your ring finger.* Then play the pattern and licks below:

G Blues—Second Pattern

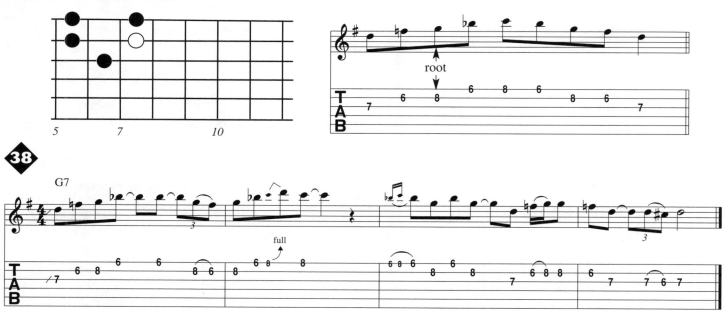

▶ *To play the third blues box, play the F formation of the IV chord.* For example, in the key of G, play the F formation/C chord at the 8th fret, because C is the IV chord of G. Then play the following scale and licks:

G Blues—Third Pattern

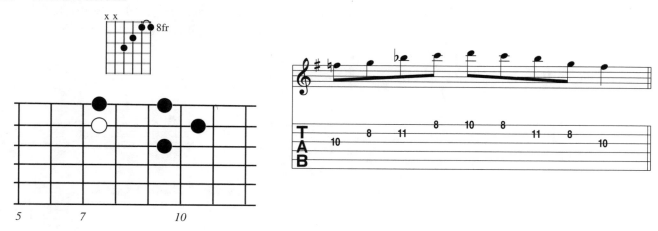

DO IT!

▶ *Play blues licks (using all three boxes) in bluesy tunes like the jazzy 12-bar and 8-bar tunes that follow:*

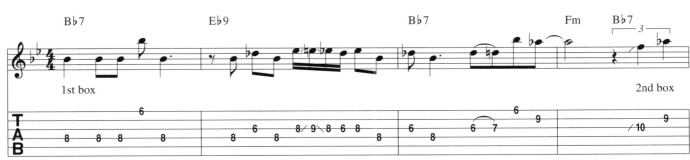

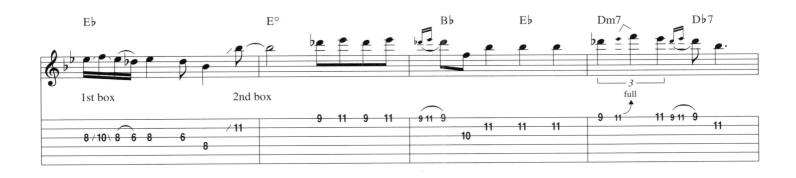

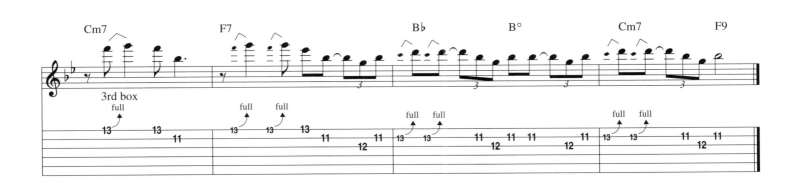

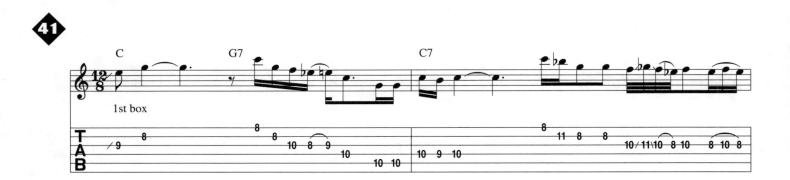

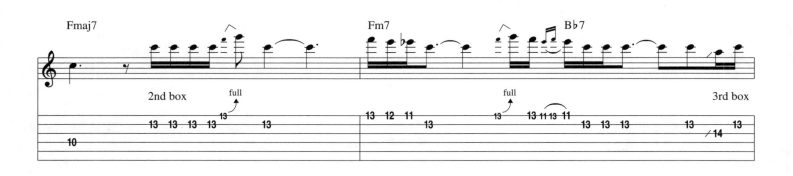

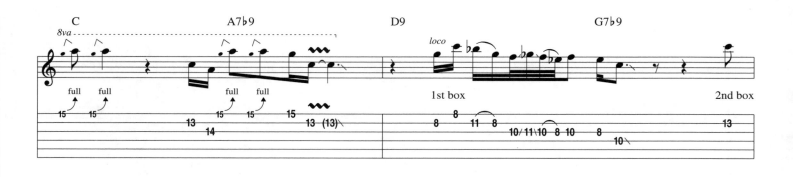

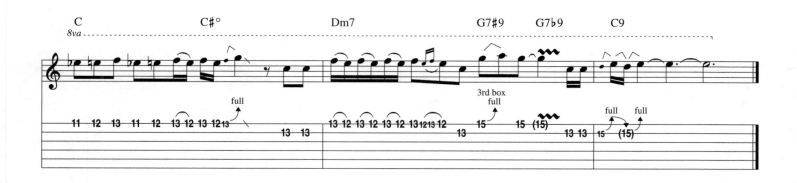

► *Play blues licks in circle-of-fifths chord progressions:*

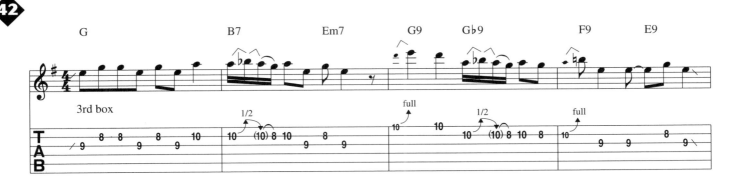

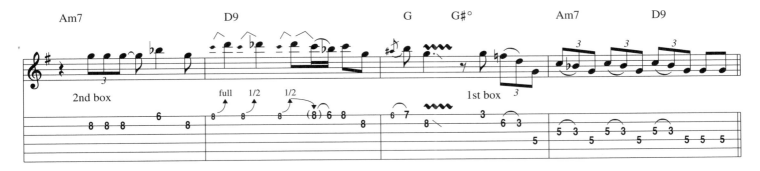

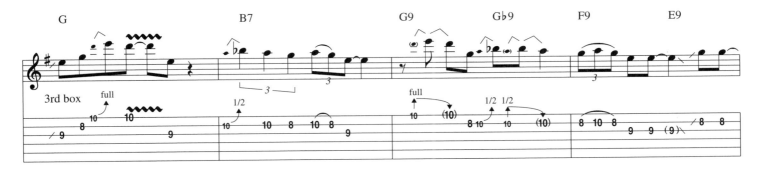

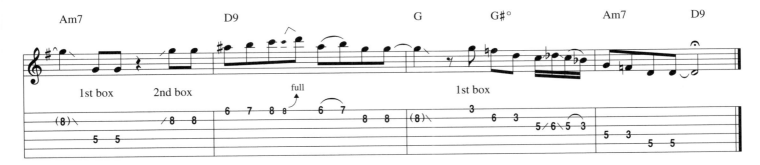

► *Play blues licks when "cycling" back to the I chord* (during a ii–V–I, VI–ii– V–I, etc.), even if the blues scales don't work with the rest of the song.

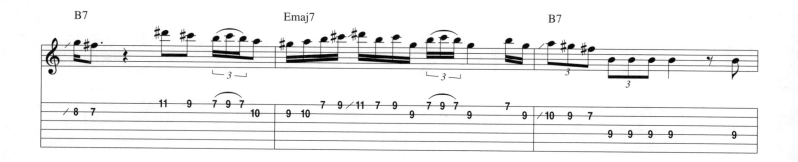

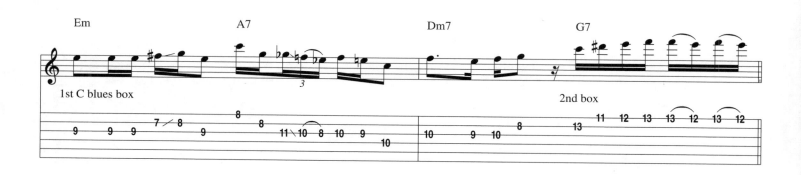

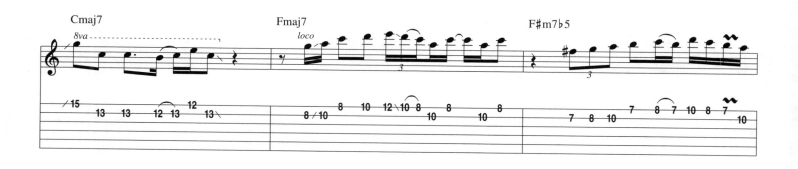

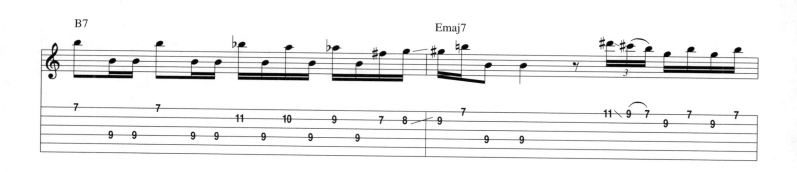

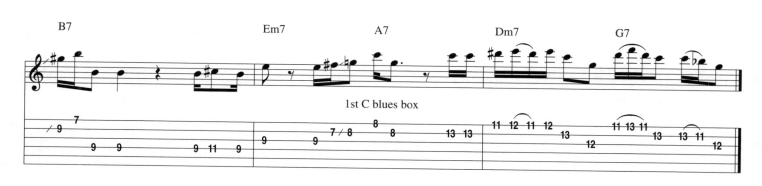

> *When the blues boxes sound inappropriate, you can use the first two boxes **THREE FRETS LOWER than the actual key.*** It changes your minor (blues) pentatonic scale to a major pentatonic scale:

SUMMING UP—NOW YOU KNOW...

> *Three moveable blues boxes and some licks that go with them*

> *How to use them in a blues, in a circle-of-fifths progression, or when "cycling back to I" in a non-bluesy tune*

> *How to play substitute blues scales, three frets below the actual key, when the given blues scales don't fit a song*

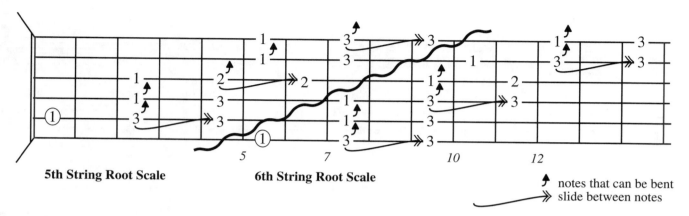

5th String Root Scale   **6th String Root Scale**

♪ notes that can be bent
≫ slide between notes

WHY?

► These versatile scales offer yet another single-note soloing approach. They can sound appropriate in bluesy and non-blues tunes.

WHAT?

► *There are two B♭ pentatonic scales in* **ROADMAP #11**. One starts on the 5th string, the other starts on the 6th string.

► *The long arrows indicate slides, short arrows can be stretched.*

► *This pentatonic scale consists of 1, 2, 3, 5 and 6.* To remember how it sounds, hum the "My Girl" riff.

► *You can play a sliding scale throughout a tune, or change scales with the changing key centers.*

HOW?

► *Play both sliding scales over and over to become familiar with them:*

C Sliding Scale (5th string root)

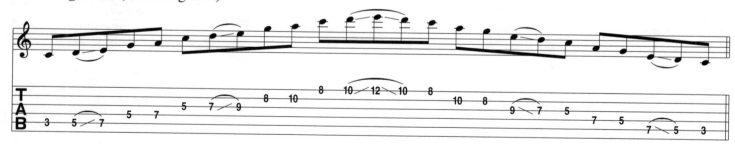

C Sliding Scale (6th string root)

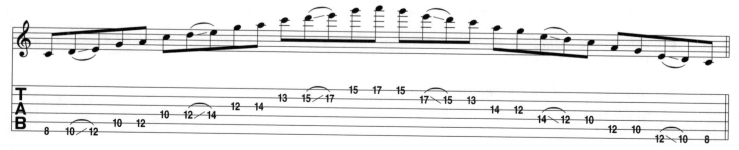

DO IT!

▶ *Play sliding scale licks throughout the "Rhythm changes" or standard I–vi–ii–V changes.*

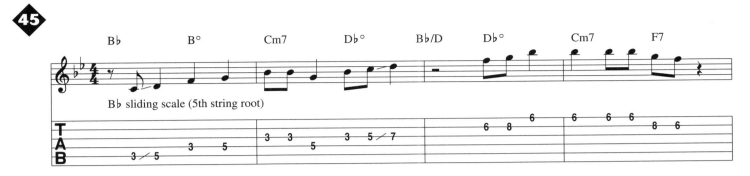

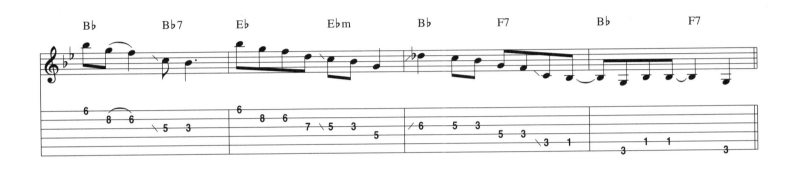

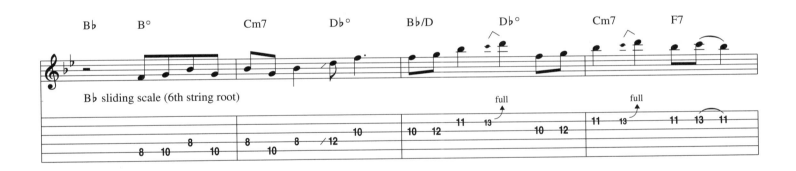

► *Use the "key centers" concept and change sliding scales,* as in the example below, which is the standard bridge from the last chapter. The Bridge starts in the key of B, modulates to D, then goes back to the main 8-bar phrase in the key of G.

46

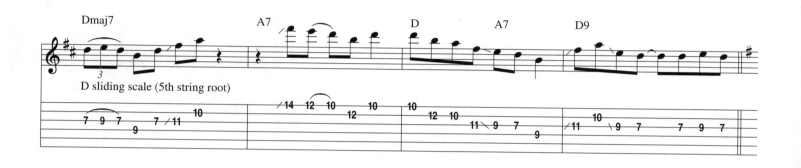

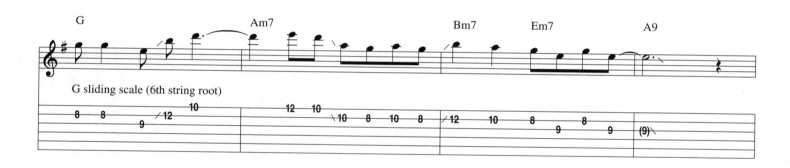

SUMMING UP—NOW YOU KNOW...

► *Two major pentatonic scales for each key*

► *How to use them to ad lib solos*

DIMINISHED AND AUGMENTED SCALES

#12

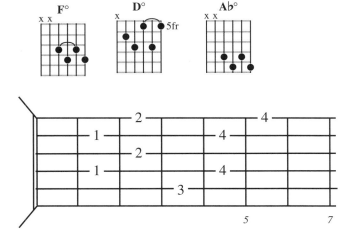

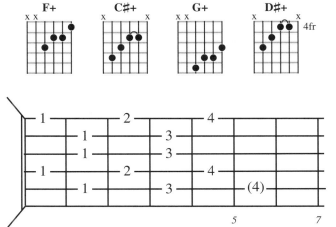

F° Scale　　　　　　　　　　　**F+ Scale**

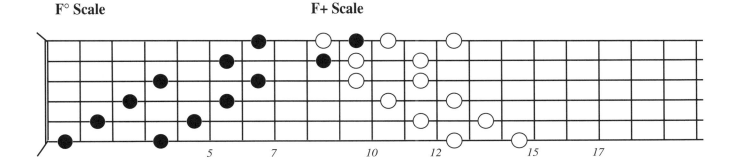

WHY?

▶ Just a hint of these scales, mixed in with major and pentatonics, makes your soloing much more interesting and jazzy.

WHAT?

▶ **ROADMAP #12** *shows an F diminished (F°) scale and an F augmented (F+) scale.* The numbers are fingering suggestions.

▶ *The diminished scale ascends by minor 3rds.* As you ascend the scale, your fretting hand goes up the fretboard in an odd, spider-like motion (as shown in the long fretboard, above).

▶ *The augmented scale ascends by whole steps.* As you ascend the scale your fretting hand goes down the fretboard, almost a reverse of the diminished pattern (see above).

▶ You can create many scale patterns from the long fretboard, above. *The F scales in the two smaller fretboards (above) are handy because they relate to the indicated chord shapes.*

HOW?

▶ ***You can use these scales whenever the appropriate chord occurs.*** Play a C diminished scale for a C° chord, an A augmented scale for A+.

▷ Start the scale from the appropriate note:

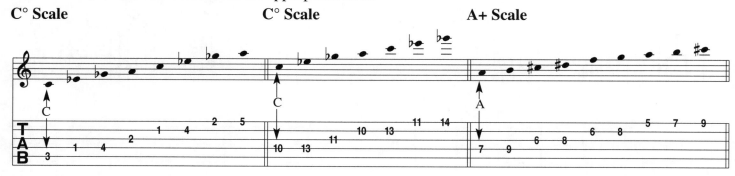

▷ Relate the scale to the appropriate chord:

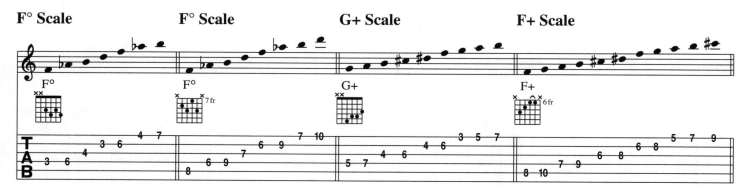

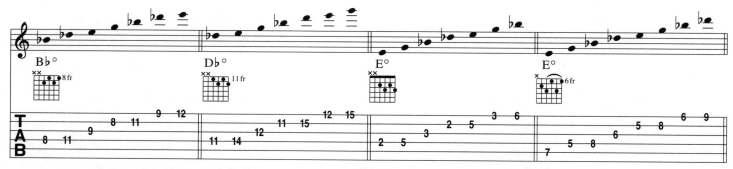

▶ ***The diminished chord repeats every three frets, so you can use the diminished scale that matches any of its "repeats."*** Where a G° scale is appropriate, you can substitute a B♭°, D♭° or E° scale.

You can substitute these chords (and their scales) for one another.

Here's another way to look at the same idea: the diminished chord can be named by any of its four notes (1, ♭3, ♭5, 6). Cdim can be called E♭°, G♭°, or A°. Therefore, you can play an E♭°, G♭° or A° scale anywhere you would play a C° scale.

► *The augmented chord repeats every four frets, so you can use the augmented scale that matches any of its "repeats."*

F+ Scales

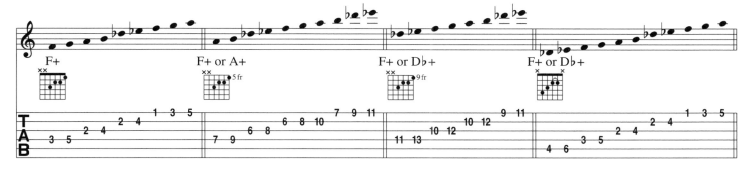

You can substitute these chords (and their scales) for one another.

► *You can use the augmented scale when a 7th chord occurs.* Play a G+ scale for a G7, G9, G13, etc. Start the scale on any G note, or on the flatted seventh, F:

G+ Scales

You can instantly find an augmented scale by relating it to a 7th chord shape:

D+ Scales

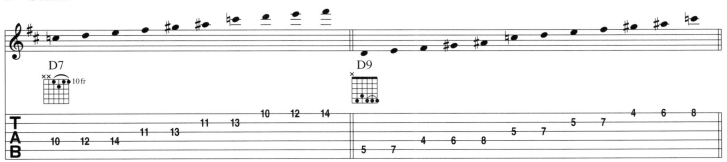

► *When a 7th chord occurs, you can use the diminished scale a half-step (one fret) higher.* Play a G♯dim scale for a G7, G9 etc. You can find the appropriate scale by relating it to a 7th chord:

D♯° Scales (for a D7 chord)

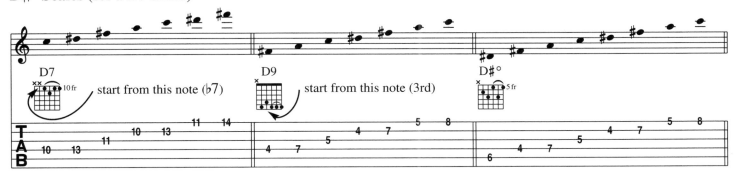

DO IT!

▶ *Play diminished scale/licks in these standard progressions, when a diminished or 7th chord occurs:*

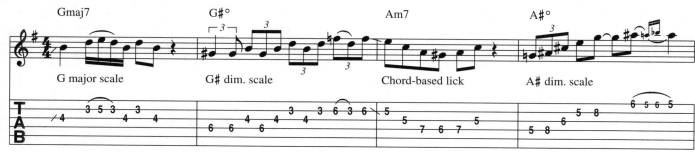

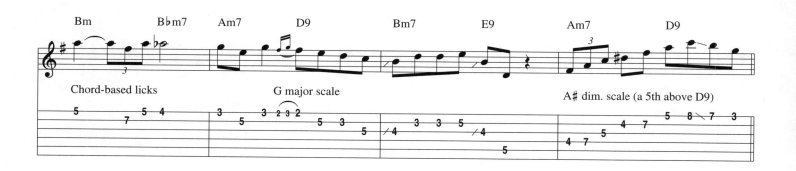

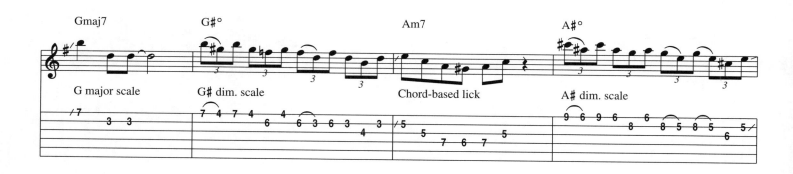

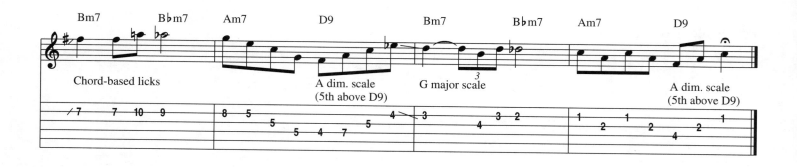

"I Got Rhythm" Bridge

▶ *Play augmented scale/licks in these standard progressions, when an augmented or 7th chord occurs:*

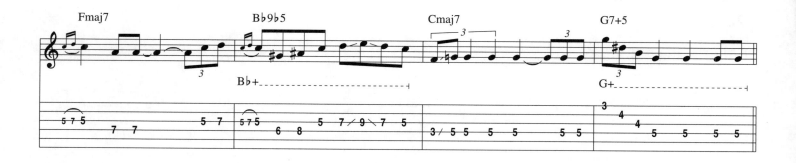

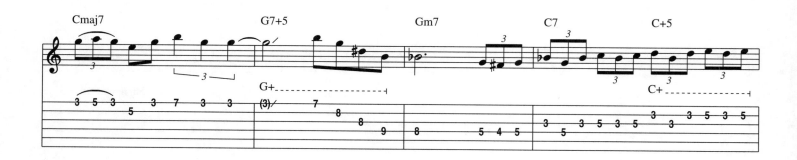

50
"Honeysuckle Rose" Bridge

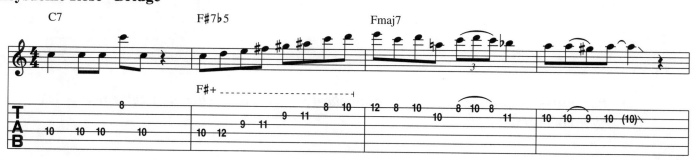

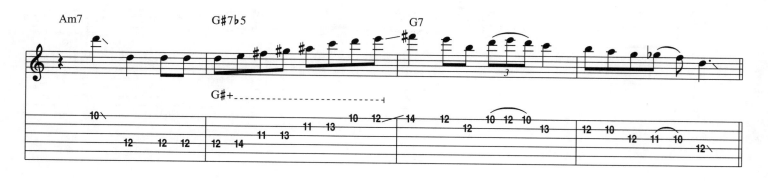

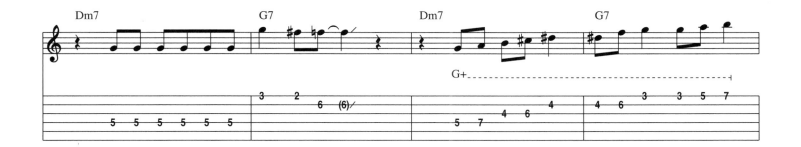

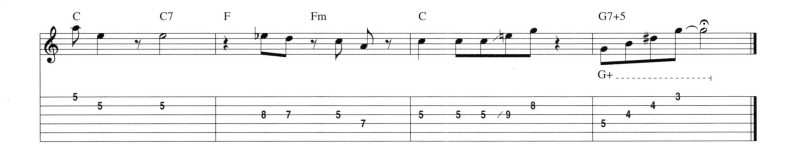

SUMMING UP—NOW YOU KNOW...

▶ *How to play diminished scales*

▶ *How to play augmented scales*

▶ *How to use these scales when a 7th chord occurs*

▶ *How to play multiple diminished or augmented scales in any instance* (e.g., by substituting Bb°, Db° or E° scales for a G° chord)

♪ USING THE PRACTICE TRACKS

TRACK #1 is a 12-bar blues in G. The first time around, the soloist uses the first G blues box. The second time, first and second G blues box licks are played. The third time, blues box licks are mixed with chord-based and diminished licks. The chord progression is:

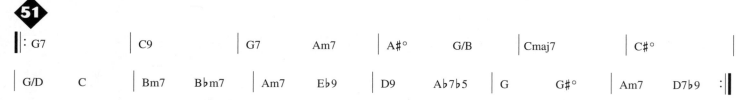

51

‖: G7 | C9 | G7 Am7 | A♯° G/B | Cmaj7 | C♯° |

| G/D C | Bm7 B♭m7 | Am7 E♭9 | D9 A♭7♭5 | G G♯° | Am7 D7♭9 :‖

TRACK #2 is an 8-bar blues in E♭. The first time around, the soloist uses E♭ blues boxes. The second time, diminished and augmented scales are also used during the diminished and augmented chords. The chord progression is:

52

‖: E♭maj7 B♭7+5 | B♭m7 A7 | A♭maj7 B♭m7 A♭/C A♭ | A° |

| E♭maj7 C7♭9+5 | F9 B♭7♭9+5 | E♭9 A♭7 | E♭maj7 B♭7+5 :‖

TRACK #3 is an AABA tune: an 8-bar A section is played twice, followed by an 8-bar bridge (B). Then the A part is repeated once more, to complete one cycle of the progression (AABA). The tune is a variant of the "rhythm changes" in B♭. The soloist uses pentatonic (sliding) scales during the A parts. The bridge has some diminished scales, played over 7th chords. The second time around, the bridge consists of chord-based licks.

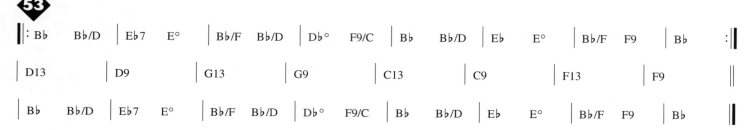

53

‖: B♭ B♭/D | E♭7 E° | B♭/F B♭/D | D♭° F9/C | B♭ B♭/D | E♭ E° | B♭/F F9 | B♭ :‖

| D13 | D9 | G13 | G9 | C13 | C9 | F13 | F9 ‖

| B♭ B♭/D | E♭7 E° | B♭/F B♭/D | D♭° F9/C | B♭ B♭/D | E♭ E° | B♭/F F9 | B♭ ‖

TRACK #4 Is an AABA tune; the A part is the scalewise progression mentioned in **ROADMAP #5**, and the B part is the "Honeysuckle Rose bridge." The solo is built on G major scales during the A sections. The bridge begins in the key of B, so the solo shifts to B major scales. As the key centers change, so does the soloing, as indicated below:

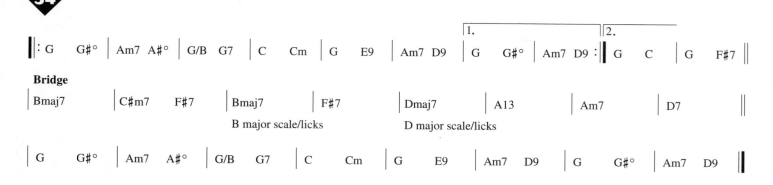

54

‖: G G♯° | Am7 A♯° | G/B G7 | C Cm | G E9 | Am7 D9 |¹· G G♯° | Am7 D9 :‖²· G C | G F♯7 ‖

Bridge

| Bmaj7 | C♯m7 F♯7 | Bmaj7 | F♯7 | Dmaj7 | A13 | Am7 | D7 ‖

                 B major scale/licks   D major scale/licks

| G G♯° | Am7 A♯° | G/B G7 | C Cm | G E9 | Am7 D9 | G G♯° | Am7 D9 ‖